Good For Me
Fruit

Sally Hewitt

WAYLAND

Notes for Teachers and Parents

Good for Me is a series of books that looks at ways of helping children to develop a positive approach to eating. You can use the books to help children make healthy choices about what they eat and drink as an important part of a healthy lifestyle.

Look for fruit when you go shopping.
• Look at the different types of fruit in your local supermarket.
• Read the ingredients on packets to see if the food contains fruit.
• Buy something new. Have fun preparing it and eating it with children.

Talk about different food groups and how we need to eat a variety of food from each group every day.
• Fruit is packed with vitamins and minerals and fibre.
• Talk about the ways vitamins, minerals and fibre help to keep us strong and healthy.

Talk about how we feel when we are healthy and the things we can do to help us to stay healthy.
• Eat food that is good for us.
• Drink plenty of water.
• Enjoy fresh air and exercise.
• Sleep well.

First published in 2007 by Wayland
Reprinted in 2007
Copyright © Wayland 2007
Wayland
338 Euston Road
London NW1 3BH

Wayland Australia
Hachette Children's Books
Level 17/207 Kent Street
Sydney NSW 2000

Produced by Tall Tree Ltd
Editor: Jon Richards
Designer: Ben Ruocco
Consultant: Sally Peters

British Library Cataloguing in Publication Data
Hewitt, Sally, 1949–
   Fruit. – (Good for me!)
   1. Fruit – Juvenile literature 2. Fruit in human nutrition
   – Juvenile literature 3. Health – Juvenile literature
   I. Title
   641.3'4

ISBN-13: 9780750250009

Printed in China
Wayland is a division of Hachette Children's Books,
a Hachette Livre UK Company

Picture credits:
Cover top Alamy/Megapress, bottom Dreamstime.com/Liz van Steenburgh,
1 and 21 centre left Dreamstime.com/Glenn Walker,
4l Dreamstime.com/Steve Degehardt, 4r Dreamstime.com,
5 Dreamstime.com/Ulina Tauer, 6 Dreamstime.com/Kathleen Melis,
7 Dreamstime.com/Magdalena Kucova, 8 Dreamstime.com/Jan Matoska,
9 Dreamstime.com/Lana Langois, 10 Dreamstime.com/Antoine Beyeler,
11 Alamy/Simon Rawles, 12 Alamy/Megapress,
13 Dreamstime.com/Juan Lobo, 14 Dreamstime.com/Marek Kosmal,
15l Dreamstime.com/Marek Tihelka, 15r Dreamstime.com,
16 Dreamstime.com, 17 Dreamstime.com/Paul Morley,
18 Dreamstime.com/Leonid Nyshko, 19 Dreamstime.com/Max Blain,
20 middle Dreamstime.com/Liz van Steenburgh, bottom left
Dreamstime.com/Melissa Dockstader, bottom middle Dreamstime.com/Tyler
Olsen, bottom right Lorna Ainger, 21 top middle Dreamstime.com/Ryan
Jorgensen, upper centre Dreamstime.com/Tyler Olson, centre right
Dreamstime.com/Pamela Hodson, centre Dreamstime.com/Andrzej Tokarski,
bottom left Dreamstime.com/Olga Lyubkina, bottom middle
Dreamstime.com/Jack Schiffer, bottom right Dreamstime.com,
23 Alamy/Megapress

Contents

Good for me

Everyone needs to eat food and drink water to live, grow and be **healthy**. All the food we eat comes from animals and plants. Fruit is food from plants.

Fruit comes in all different shapes, sizes and colours, including green apples and red cherries.

You can pick your
own fruit, such as
strawberries, at
local farms.

Fruit is grown in **orchards**, on farms
and in gardens. It needs rain and
sunshine to grow and become **ripe**.
This means that the fruit is ready to eat.

Vitamins, minerals and fibre

Fruit is full of **vitamins** and **minerals**. Every part of your body needs vitamins and minerals to be healthy and to fight **germs**.

Eating crunchy fruit helps to keep your teeth strong and healthy.

Fruit contains natural sugar that gives you **energy**. It is also full of **fibre** that helps your body to get rid of unwanted food.

Oranges contain lots of vitamin C, which can help to stop you catching colds.

Lunch box

Squeeze fresh oranges for a healthy drink at lunchtime.

Fruit from trees

Many trees produce fruit in order to protect their **seeds**, including apples, cherries and pears. We grow fruit trees in farms, called orchards.

Cherry trees grow flowers, called blossom, before they grow fruit.

Pears and apples contain seeds inside them, which are surrounded by the hard fruit.

Fruit is juicy because it stores food for a plant's seeds. When the fruit falls from a tree, the seed inside starts to grow. The fruit gives the seed the food it needs to grow.

Lunch box

Mix together some chopped apples, chopped celery, walnuts, raisins and mayonnaise to make a Waldorf salad.

9

All over the world

Fruit is sent all over the world inside trucks, boats and planes. These vehicles have special fridges and freezers that keep the fruit fresh. This means that you can eat fruit that has travelled thousands of kilometres.

This pink, spiky fruit is called rambutan. It comes from Thailand.

You can eat bananas that have come from Africa, pineapples from the Philippines and kiwi fruit that has come from New Zealand.

Bananas are green and unripe when they are packed and shipped. The bananas turn yellow when they are ripe.

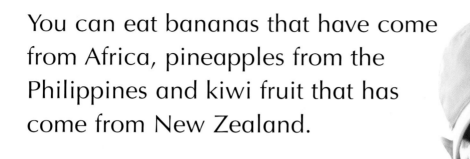

Lunch box

Make a fruit salad from all over world:
Use mangoes from India, blueberries from Canada and oranges from Spain.

Growing fruit

Fruit grows on plants of all shapes and sizes. Oranges and lemons grow on trees, while strawberries and blackberries grow on bushes.

Blackberries and blueberries grow wild in cooler countries. You can pick them off bushes, but ask an adult before you do.

Grapes grow on plants called vines. These are grown in long rows that make the grapes easy to pick.

On fruit farms, the plants are looked after as they grow. The fruit is picked by hand or by special machines.

Lunch box

Add a slice of pineapple to a cheese sandwich for your lunch box.

Eating fruit

Fruit has **skin** that protects it and makes it easy to carry as a snack. Some fruit has skin that is good to eat, while other fruit has skin that is too tough to chew.

Oranges are covered in a thick skin. Inside are juicy, bite-sized pieces.

Fruits of different colours contain different vitamins and minerals. Eat fruit of all colours to get as many vitamins and minerals as you can.

Lunch box

Put pieces of coloured fruit onto skewers. See how many different colours you can use.

Vitamin A for healthy skin is found in orange mangoes. A mineral called magnesium for strong bones is found in green kiwi fruit.

Buying and storing

We can buy fresh fruit at a greengrocer, a market or a supermarket. Fruit with tough skins, such as oranges and lemons, will keep longer than soft fruit, such as peaches or plums.

Fresh fruit is delivered to market stalls and shops every day.

Fruit can be dried in the sunshine or inside a special machine called a **dehydrator**.

Fruit can be frozen, canned or dried so that it lasts longer. Frozen fruit stored in a freezer lasts for about three months. Canned fruit will last for more than a year.

Lunch box

Add some dried fruit and slices of banana to your breakfast cereal.

17

Cooked fruit

Fruit needs to be cooked carefully. If fruit is cooked for too long it loses some of its goodness and will contain fewer vitamins.

Fruit can be cooked with **savoury** food. Here, chicken has been cooked with lemon.

Fruit is used to fill pies, tarts and crumbles. Fresh and dried fruit can be added to muffins and biscuits to add flavour.

Lunch box

Add apples or berries mixed with a little honey to plain yogurt for your lunch box.

Dried fruit, such as raisins and sultanas, is used to make a fruit cake.

19

Food chart

Here are some examples of food and drink that can be made using three types of fruit. Have you tried any of these?

Apple

Apple pie

Apple juice

Dried apple pieces

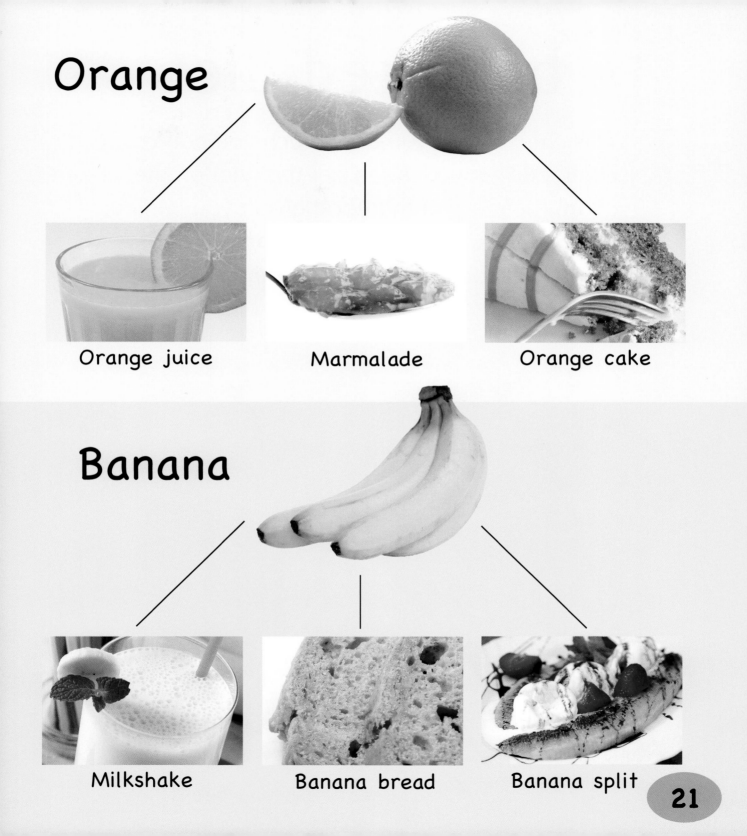

Orange

Orange juice

Marmalade

Orange cake

Banana

Milkshake

Banana bread

Banana split

21

A balanced diet

This chart shows you how much you can eat of each food group. The larger the area on the chart, the more of that food group you can eat. For example, you can eat a lot of fruit and vegetables, but only a little oil and sweets. Drink plenty of water every day, too.

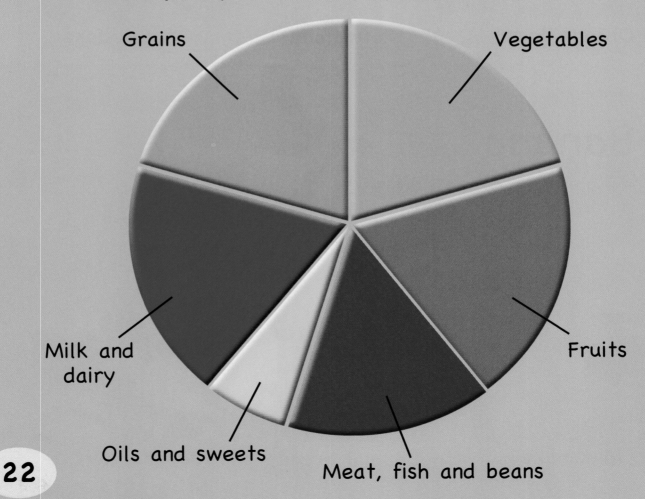

Grains

Vegetables

Milk and dairy

Fruits

Oils and sweets

Meat, fish and beans

Our bodies also need exercise to stay healthy. You should spend at least 20 minutes exercising every day so that your body stays fit and healthy.

Walking to school every day is a great way to exercise.

Glossary

Dehydrator A machine used to dry fruit.

Energy The power we need to live and grow.

Fibre The rough part of fruit. It helps your body to get rid of any unwanted food.

Germs Tiny creatures that can be harmful and can make you ill.

Healthy When you are fit and not ill.

Minerals Important substances that are found in food. Calcium is a mineral that helps to build strong bones.

Orchards Fields of fruit trees.

Ripe Something that is ready to eat.

Savoury A food that does not taste sweet.

Seeds Parts of plants that grow to form new plants.

Skin The outside layer of fruit. Oranges have a thick skin called peel. Apples have a thin skin that we can eat.

Vitamins Substances found in food that help our bodies stay healthy.

Index